Waiting for My Left Foot
A Short Story

Marie Ceribelli

Dedicated to my friend, Ann Marie
and to all those who suffer from ALS.

"Patience is not simply the ability to wait -
it's how we behave while we're waiting."
(Joyce Meyer)

Introduction

I broke my left foot when summer began, possibly making it one of my worst summers ever, a summer bummer. I twisted my ankle on a sneaker that was left on a step. The twist caused the breakage of two bones, the third and fifth metatarsal bones in my foot. I immediately stood up and walked on it thinking it could not possibly be broken. Within one hour of my fall, the foot became swollen at which time I proceeded to go to the emergency room to have x-rays taken.

I took off from work that first week and went to the podiatrist as soon as I possibly could. He told me to stay off the foot and to take a short leave from work and collect disability insurance for approximately one month. I was stubborn and chose not to listen, as I felt that I would just sit at my desk. I was told not to stand, walk or drive. I didn't realize how much pressure I was putting on my foot until I had x-rays retaken after one month. After one month there was no improvement, resulting in me having to listen to the doctor and take off from work. I had to regroup and figure out how to stay off my foot completely. I had to constantly think about how to maneuver without using my left foot. I was determined to remain in bed for half of the day and then I moved to a chair for the remainder of the day. I was vigilant with my foot soaks and in using my Exogen ultrasound bone healing system. I got up only a few times a day to use the bathroom or to eat a meal. Sometimes I ate in bed or on the couch, so I would not have to move.

I remember feeling angry and disappointed. I

then switched my thoughts to my aunt and my

cousin who were fighting cancer during that same

time. This was nothing compared to what they

had to endure. I felt so much compassion for

them both and hoped for the best outcome and

results. I was grateful that all my broken foot

required was time to heal without requiring

surgery or any other treatment. I was also

grateful for wearing a removable cast, as it was

nice not having to sleep with it on my leg.

I had hoped to be better before the Fall semester began, as I was so close to graduating and didn't want to delay it. I decided to write about my experience while I sat around waiting for my left foot to heal, repair and mend.

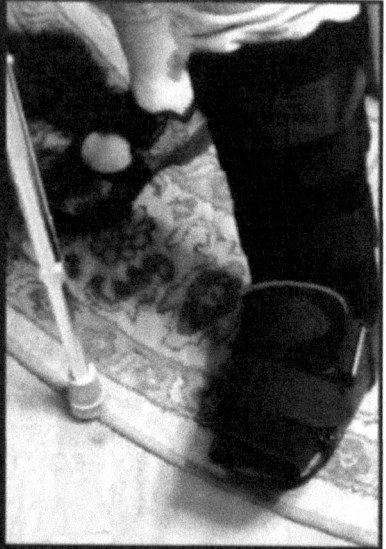

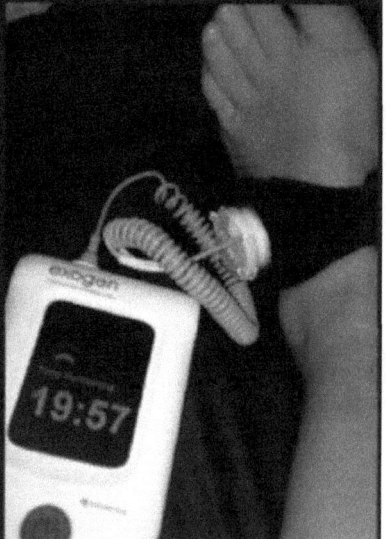

Waiting

As I sat with my broken foot, I could not help but think and wait. I was waiting for the bones to heal and as I waited I had to stay off my foot. Staying off my foot has caused more episodes of waiting. I waited for someone to come home and cook dinner; I waited for my laundry to be done and for someone to come by and empty the dishwasher. My husband and children had to go to the stores and bank for me and fetch me things that were only a few feet away. As exciting as that may appear to be for

8

some, that excitement wore off for my family and I after the first week. It became a little annoying to have to ask someone to hand me something that was not too far away. I sat and waited day in and day out.

This broken foot had caused me to become disabled, leaving me with a new appreciation for my foot like never before. It was so difficult to do what seemed to be so simple, such as: walking, bathing and dressing. I learned not to wait for the last minute to use the bathroom, as it took so much longer to get there. I had to constantly stay focused on how not to put any pressure on my foot. I approached the shower stool on one leg, then sat without slipping. I learned how to balance myself. I could not work and I did not get paid while I was out of work, which left me with more appreciation for my paycheck, as it was more than what disability insurance paid me.

My first few days at home, I organized and deleted many photographs on my technical devices to make more storage space. I also created many Pic Collages (an app that allows you to create amazing collages using your photos, stickers, text and frames) and Flipagrams (an app that helps you create short photo-video stories set to music). I had to make sure that everything I needed for the day was right beside me, such as my iPhone, iPad, remote controls for the TV, the Apple TV and the ultrasound device for my foot. I had a blanket, pillows, books, magazines, tissues and water nearby as well. I was home alone from Monday through Friday. I waited for anyone to walk through the door, just to have some conversation about their day. I did plenty of reading and writing during that time. I also watched many movies and television shows. I also spent my days soaking my foot several times a day and twice a day I used the ultrasound device on my broken bones. I found myself conversing with the dog, I actually enjoyed snuggling up with her. I became more in tune with the outside noises and the inside creaks of my old house. I heard the sound of landscapers and construction workers on a daily basis. The sound of cars passing by and airplanes and helicopters flying over my house became so profound. I could hear the air conditioner go on and off. I knew when it was garbage day as the sound of the garbage truck seemed so much louder. I heard dogs barking and birds chirping like never before. It was so quiet otherwise. I could not wait to hear the mail drop into my mailbox, hoping for something good to come. I had applied for a temporary handicap parking permit and waited for it to arrive. What made this so difficult was the fact that I felt well and not sick at all. When you feel ill you don't mind sleeping and lying around. It became frustrating as the weeks passed by. After six weeks, the x-rays of my foot started to show a slight improvement.

As the second month began, I could see and feel the physical change in muscle tone in my left foot and leg due to the lack of exercise. My leg became thin and mushy and felt numb. I looked forward to going online where I did get to enjoy summer through the eyes of my Facebook friends. I survived that summer by living vicariously through my Facebook friends and family. During that summer, New York Giant's Michael Strahan was inducted into the NFL Hall of Fame and actors, Angelina Jolie and Brad Pitt finally got married, and sadly and suddenly, Robin Williams and Joan Rivers passed away. I remembered all the happiness and laughter they brought into my life, their deaths brought me so much sadness and sorrow. I felt grateful for DVD's so that I can continue to watch them and laugh and someday share their movies with my grandchildren. Their legacies will live on for generations to come. Lauren Bacall, one of cinema's most glamorous actresses also passed

away that summer. I stayed very well informed

on local and world news. The world was horrified

when American journalists, James Foley and

Steven Sotloff were beheaded by ISIS, a

militant Islamic group, and their brutal

beheadings were posted on YouTube. The world

outside my safe and humble abode was being

terrorized and people were scared. The world

kept on spinning as my world stood still. I found

myself waiting and hoping for someone to come

by and visit. It took eight weeks for the bones to

heal, followed by physical therapy. I had to continue wearing the removable cast and I had to be evaluated by the physical therapist in order to receive my "return to work" letter. I looked forward to getting back to my normal routine.

During the third month, I became hopeful that I would soon be able to babysit my grandson and to once again be able to walk to the park with him. Babysitting was not possible during the first two months. I supervised my husband from the couch when he was needed to babysit. I got an occasional hug and kiss from my grandson when he came over to me. I was also hoping to get

back to work, as I began to miss my workplace

and my coworkers. I missed school and hoped to

be able to start the next semester on time. I

remember speaking to my cousin, who had had

several eye surgeries that summer, as a result of

his diabetes. He was slowly losing his vision. I

had thought of him as he had been bed-ridden

many times because of his ailments. When he

asked me about my foot, I felt embarrassed and

ashamed to talk about it to him. I could not wait

to get back to exercising, as diabetes is not what I want in my future. Once again, I was grateful that all I had was a broken foot.

When I began physical therapy, it felt so good to remove that boot and walk barefoot once again. Taking a shower while standing was invigorating! I had to learn how to walk properly, this is known as gait therapy. All the muscles in my foot and leg needed to be strengthened. All my tendons and ligaments haven't been used in three months. As I walked it was slightly painful and sore, therefore, I had to approach this slowly and not overdue it. I had physical therapy twice a week for two months. I had to workout twice a day at home and continue with the foot soaks and ultrasound device. I had to put aside an hour each morning before work and an hour after work for my workout and foot care. The whole process took four months before I was able to wear a shoe or a sneaker again. I did miss my first week of classes, but I kept in touch with my professors via email. I did my assignments from home until I was able to attend class. In celebration of my newly healed foot, while sitting on a stool, I found myself preparing and cooking my favorite middle eastern delights: yabra' (stuffed grape leaves), kibbeh bissaneeyeh (two layers of lamb chopmeat with a meat stuffing in between those two layers), lahim biajeen (open meat pies) and balawa (rich, sweet pastry made of layers of filo filled with chopped walnuts and sweetened and held together with a syrup). I had a new found appreciation for my grandmother and the women of her generation, as there is so much preparation in making these foods and it is very time consuming. I could not wait to share this feast with my family. It all worked out and I was thrilled to have my life back, the way it was prior to breaking my foot.

Foot Baths

I have learned to take better care of my feet since this ordeal. I continue with the foot soaks and I do them at least twice a day. My feet are much healthier and smoother. I do a fifteen minute foot soak before work in the morning and before bed every night now and I find it extremely relaxing. Foot baths help improve circulation and also help prevent sweaty feet.

> *Immersing your feet in a tub of warm water, even without anything extra in it, is a nice way to relax after a long day. A foot soak soothes your muscles, hydrates your skin and can relieve aches and pains due to standing for hours or walking in uncomfortable shoes. Plus, letting your feet sit in their own bath can help reduce*

swelling and prevent bacteria from settling into blisters and cuts or under toe nails. And while a little rough skin helps protect our feet, if you're prone to developing thick calluses, softening them in a soak makes them easier to exfoliate— precisely the reason why most pedicures begin by submerging your feet into warm water.

There are some additions, however, that can enhance your healing foot soak. Consider these options when caring for your hard-working feet:

Epsom Salt Foot Soaks

A combination of magnesium and sulfate, Epsom salt is a compound that can help flush toxins and heavy metals from your skin's cells, reduce inflammation, increase circulation and ease muscle cramps and joint pain. As your feet absorb the magnesium, pain-reducing ions are released, relaxing your muscles and nerves and helping them function properly by regulating your electrolyte levels. The sulfate targets any harmful substances that need to be eliminated from your body.

Epsom salt can also quell foot odor, help heal fungus or ingrown nails, and soothe dry skin.

You'll find this healing salt at most drug stores and pharmacies. In a standard size tub, dissolve one cup of Epsom salt in warm water and soak your feet for 10 to 15 minutes. (*http://www.canyonranch.com/your-health/whole-beauty/nurture-yourself/your-home-spa/the-healing-benefits-foot-soaks#fbid=kfrbq2T2_OF*)

I highly recommend daily foot soaks and I believe this is a good habit to have. Soaking my feet was one of the most valuable and relaxing lessons that I have learned while waiting for my foot to heal.

ALS

The summer videos of the ALS ice bucket challenge flooded Facebook and I was glad to see that debilitating disease get some recognition. What is ALS?

Amyotrophic lateral sclerosis (ALS)—also referred to as motor neuron disease (MND), Charcot disease, and, in the United States, Lou Gehrig's disease—is a neurodegenerative disease with various causes. It is characterized by muscle spasticity, rapidly progressive weakness due to muscle atrophy, difficulty in speaking (dysarthria), swallowing (dysphagia), and breathing (dyspnea). ALS is the most common of the five motor

neuron diseases. The disorder causes

muscle weakness and atrophy

throughout the body due to the

degeneration of the upper and lower

motor neurons. Individuals affected

by the disorder may ultimately lose

the ability to initiate and control all

voluntary movement, although bladder

and bowel function and the muscles

responsible for eye movement are

usually spared until the final stages of

the disease. (Wikipedia)

Six months prior to the ALS ice bucket

challenge, I had written a paper about ALS for

my neuroscience class. I created my own case

study which was based on a friend of mine. This

disease took her life when she was thirty years

old, eleven months after her baby was born. In

less than one year from being diagnosed, she was

dead. It seemed that the hormonal and chemical

changes in her body during pregnancy brought

her disease to life. It took the doctor a few

months before he was able to make his diagnosis.

Her disease progressed rapidly and I

remembered how she suffered and how awful it

was for her not being able to hold or care for

her baby. She was always very energetic and

athletic and this crippling disease tortured her.

Her family and friends were horrified as they

watched her demise. It was a joint venture, as

everyone took shifts to help care for her and her

baby. I thought more about ALS and how

horrible it must be not to be able to move a

muscle. A person with ALS is unable to move or

change position while lying in bed and is not able

to speak or scratch an itch. A simple task such as

changing the TV channel with the remote control

or dialing a number on the telephone is not

possible if you are a person who suffers with

ALS. Brushing your teeth or hair are

impossibilities. Getting dressed is only possible

if someone dresses you. Eye movement is all

there is. As I sat with my broken foot, I

imagined what it would be like to suffer from

ALS. I attempted not moving a muscle or

changing my position, just to see what it would be

like. I did not use my phone or TV remote control

for a very short time...a short time was all I

could stand, as it was extremely difficult. It was

probably more difficult because I could move,

but I wanted to better understand an ALS

patient. I feel compassion for ALS patients and

their family members and friends. I am hoping

that all those donations received from

the ice bucket challenge will help create enough

revenue to fund the necessary research to find a

treatment or a cure.

My Caretaker

My husband provided and cared for me

during that time, as he always did. The only

difference was that I could no longer contribute

in the chores that we did share together. I sat

by and watched him run around, up and down the

stairs getting all the household chores

completed. He was my personal chiropractor and

masseuse, and made sure I was adjusted and

massaged regularly. He also had to run my

errands. He prepared dinner for me and the kids

after a long day at work. He was at my beck and

call for anything that I needed. His sense of

humor, patience and tolerance got us through

that crazy time. Laughter was my best

medication. "A good laugh and a long sleep are

the best cures in the doctor's book" (Irish

Proverb) We appreciated each other more than

before, leaving us feeling grateful to have one

another. He, too lost the remainder of his

summer, as he sat beside me and kept me

company. I, at times persuaded him to go out

and take a ride to a local car show. He deserved

and needed to take a break. He felt awful leaving

me, but all I was doing was sleeping and resting

and I felt it was not fair to him. Summer time

was his special time when he enjoyed his car, a

convertible Porsche Carrera 911. Driving it and

washing it were his favorite past times. I

occasionally asked him to take me for a ride.

He needed to drive it and I needed the sun

and the wind on my face. We drove to the beach and right back home because I could not walk to get to any place, but it felt so good to see the beach and smell the ocean. As we drove by, I saw kites flying and boats sailing. We also played board games to help pass the time. Caretakers have the tendency of becoming resentful, I am fortunate to say that this was not the case here. That was the extent of our summer. We both knew that this too shall pass, so we made the best out of my situation.

My Dog

My little Shi Tzu, Tiffany, became my best friend and companion. She was there for me when no else could be. When my family all headed out to work, she was a comfort to me as she laid beside me the whole day. She has human-like eyes and it was so nurturing to feel her warmth as she laid in my arms or on my lap. Her playful spirit made me laugh, as she was just so happy that I was home with her all day long, every day.

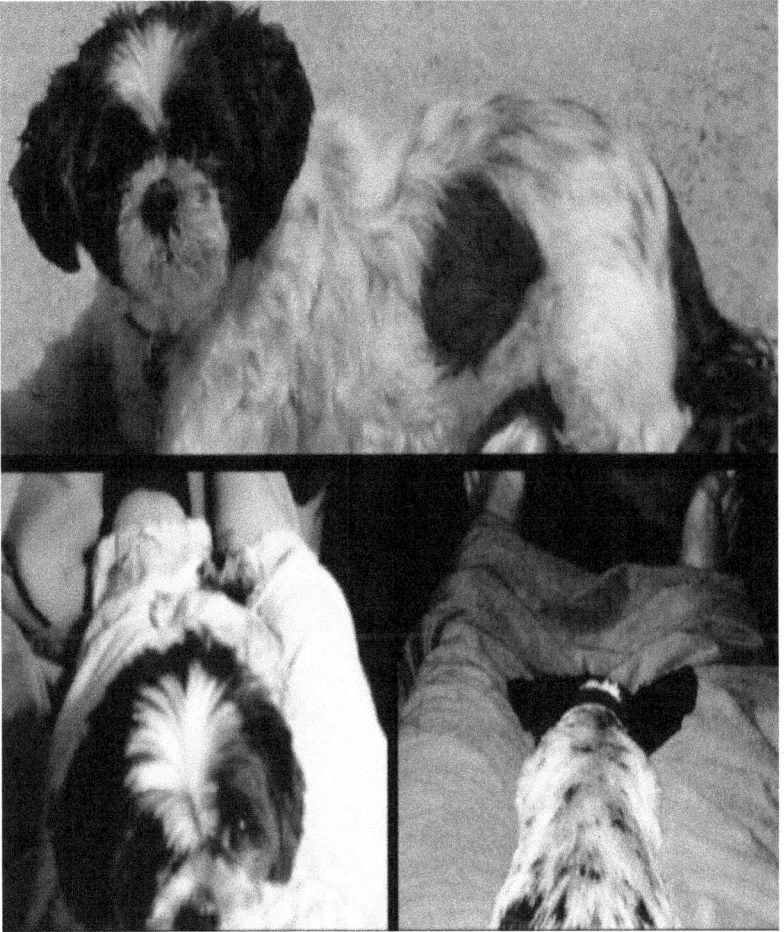

Cloudy Days

I have a new fondness for cloudy days, as the darkness of my room made it easier to sleep longer. The longer I slept the faster the day went by. I also learned that sleeping helps the healing process. It is during that time that the muscles are more relaxed making it easier for the cells to repair and mend. Hormones and the immune system also act differently while you are asleep. If the immune system does not work well, the cells cannot repair themselves. Sleeping was easier than staying awake on cloudy, dark and

gloomy days. When my husband was home on

those days, I had someone to snuggle up with.

Sunny Days

Being stuck indoors on sunny days cut me

off from all that was happening outside of my

home. I watched the news to keep up on the

weather. I got a glimpse of sunlight as it shined

through my shades and shutters during the day.

Opening my shades and shutters in the morning

was a difficult task, as I could not walk from

window to window to do so, so I left them closed.

I had to remind myself that I could not walk or

stand. My husband did not want to open them

while I slept in the morning, before he left for

work. On days when it was not too hot or humid,

I hobbled out to my lounge chair in the backyard

to soak up some of the sun's rays and absorb

some vitamin D. Vitamin D is also very crucial in

the healing process as it is needed for bone

growth and bone remodeling.

Nutrition and Exercise

It was extremely important to maintain a healthy and balanced diet that included many calcium enriched foods and supplements. I was very concerned about weight gain as I became immobile. Not to say that I was a person who worked out vigorously, but I did walk two miles in the early morning before work and I was already overweight. Hydration was extremely important as well. I made sure I kept a large bottle of ice water nearby at all times. I was not moving at all during that time, which was not good for the rest

of my body. I knew that after my foot healed I

would need to exercise in order get my body

healthier and toned. I did manage to lose a few

pounds, but I think it was all muscle that I lost.

Meditation

I had the opportunity to meditate several

hours a day, which helped me to stay relaxed,

calm and focused on the healing process.

Meditation really made me feel good inside. As I

sat outside in my backyard, I was able to take a good long look at the beautiful plants and grapevine. The colors seemed so vivid. I looked at the back of my house and thought of all the wonderful memories I have had within its walls. The two attic windows looked like eyes. It reminded me of the billboard in the "Great Gatsby" and I felt as if I was being watched. Or perhaps it was symbolic of my own two eyes as I sat and saw things like never before.

I was in awe as I laid back in my lounge

chair and looked up into the beautiful blue sky

with its white puffy clouds. The clouds

resembled fluffy pillows and I could feel the

softness of them embracing me. I would also

create images out of them. I looked at my dog as

she ran around in total contentment and then

enjoyed watching her relax as I did in complete

serenity. We both felt the sunlight on our skin

and a slight breeze on our face. Knitting,

crocheting and the art of scrapbooking would be

good forms of creative meditation during a time like this. I organized my daughter's photographs from the past year and put them into albums. I realized it was quite a year, as I flipped through her photographs and reminisced. I also learned how to play Solitaire online. In reality, waiting for my left foot to heal was a simple task, regardless of how much time it required.

I also joined a group meditation online, hosted by Oprah Winfrey and Deepak Chopra. It was a twenty-one day meditation and it was something new for me. Each day there was a new and different thought and mantra. The meditations lasted twenty minutes and after each meditation I answered four questions in an online journal. It became something that I looked forward to every day, as it left me in a euphoric state. I found this to be an exhilarating experience and I was definitely inspired by Oprah and Deepak.

Conclusion

In conclusion, I found that we spend most of our time waiting for something or someone. We wait nine months for a baby to be born. That summer I was told that I was going to be a grandmother for the second time, which created seven months' worth of time waiting for the new baby. We wait to graduate or to celebrate an important milestone. We wait for the light to turn green so we can move forward. We wait for the train or the bus to come to take us places.

We wait in line to purchase something. We wait for test grades and emails. We wait to meet our significant other. We wait for research to find a treatment or a cure. We wait and hope to learn as we grow older. We wait to heal. Once I was able to accept my situation, I became enthused and enjoyed my solitude. This was definitely an experience I shall never forget. I am thankful that my husband and I did go on vacation in May and that we did not wait until summer to get away. I am also grateful to have had the opportunity to catch up on phone calls and emails

to those I haven't spoken to in a long time. A

phone call or text message from anyone during

that time was one of the highlights of my day.

Waiting for my left foot to heal had made me

understand those with disabilities and how

difficult it is for them to function. I now have a

deeper compassion for those who suffer from

physical disabilities. My temporary disability was

nothing in comparison to what others endure on a

permanent basis. Sharing my story may seem silly

or ridiculous to some, but this experience forced me to think and learn, therefore it was not a waste of time. I am thankful for having had that time to think and learn. I am also thankful to be able to walk and run again and to be able to drive to work and school. Those mundane things such as household chores, running errands, and chasing after my grandson again, became so exciting to me. I am extremely fortunate that my broken foot was not as serious an ailment as ALS or some other debilitating disease. I am more aware of where I walk and in making sure that my path is clear with no obstructions in my

way for me to trip or fall over. I no longer wait

or postpone walking or exercising. I do it more

often now, as I appreciate being able to do so.

In the end, it wasn't a summer bummer after all,

I stopped and enjoyed life and lived it the best I

could with limitations, from where I sat and took

a good long look at life itself. It was worth

waiting for my left foot to heal properly, as it

was an important part of my life's journey.

"The only disability in life is a bad attitude."
(Scott Hamilton)